SELF-DEVELOPMENT STRATEGIES

The Five-Minute Guide to a Better You

Andrea Clarke Pratt

Published by Andrea Clarke Pratt, 2022

While every precaution has been taken in the preparation of this book, the publisher assumes responsibility for errors or omissions or for damages resulting from the use of the information contained herein.

SELF DEVELOPMENT STRATEGIES:

THE FIVE-MINUTE GUIDE TO A BETTER YOU

First edition. July 11, 2022.

Written by Andrea Clarke Pratt

Contents

"The secret of getting ahead is getting started." -Mark Twain

Are you ready to move forward in your life? Does your life feel mundane and devoid of opportunities? Well, a new day is here. A season of transformation and growth when you will discover how truly gifted you are, and your uniqueness will be revealed to the world.

Self-Development Strategies: The Five-Minute Guide to A Better You" provides the important principles needed to empower you to become a better version of yourself through focusing on important pillars of self-development such as emotions, relationships, mental and physical health, and spiritual maturity.

You will discover actionable techniques to assist you in boosting self-esteem, setting goals, developing a passion for your purpose, initiating conversations, achieving a healthier you, maintaining healthy relationships and so much more.

Are you ready to take control of your life? Procrastination is not an option; start reading this guide today and transform your life into the one you always wanted.

Self-Development: The Key to Maximizing Your Potential

"Discontent is the first step in the progress of a man or a nation." -Oscar Wilde

A clear and concise self-development plan will positively impact your life and quite possibly the lives of those most important to you. Self-development is a lifelong process. Highly successful people understand the importance of continuously improving in key areas of their lives through reading, mentorship, attending courses, and numerous other avenues.

Personal development can help you to gain a sense of ownership in various matters such as your career, health, finances, emotions, and relationships. Many companies prepare annual reports each year to summarize the mission of the company and to assess its overall performance during the year. Similarly, self-analysis should be performed regularly to define your purpose, weaknesses, and strengths and unleash your true potential. Before you begin this voyage towards self-empowerment, it is necessary to have a basic understanding of what the term self-development means.

What is Self-Development?

To put it simply, self-development involves taking the necessary steps to improve yourself. It may encompass acquiring new knowledge, skills, and abilities or overcoming negative behavior patterns.

Areas of Self Development

Attention must be given to developing emotionally, socially, mentally, spiritually, and physically if self-development is to truly be successful. Additionally, growth in developing wholesome relationships is a necessity. All these areas are important. If, for example, an individual only concentrates on developing the intellectual mind, that individual may discover eventually that all the knowledge they have cannot help them if their physical body and other areas of their lives such as relationships deteriorate. Many individuals realized this on their deathbed. If we neglect one of these areas, it may hurt our overall well-being.

Why is Self-Development Important

Self-development is important for any age group including teens, young adults, middle age, and seniors. In life, we can often get stuck in a rut, but self-development forces us to come out of our comfort zone and confront areas to achieve personal growth. With effective personal development, strengths are enhanced, and confidence is often boosted. Additionally, self-development can improve our awareness of ourselves because through self-analysis you get to know who you are, what your purpose is, and what your plans or goals are in life. Self-Development often involves moving beyond the boundaries of your comfort zone.

The following are a few bulleted points listing the importance of self-development:

- ✓ It heals relationships.
- ✓ It allows you to be proactive.
- ✓ It pushes you out of your comfort zone.

✓   It boosts your confidence.

✓   It increases self-awareness.

Beginning the Journey Towards Self-Development

Self-development begins with an introspective look at areas of weaknesses, not with a view of belittling yourself or comparing yourself negatively with others, but rather to make the necessary changes to become a better version of yourself.

It also involves self-examination of those wonderful areas you may be naturally gifted.

Perhaps those areas can be further developed to benefit you and others in immeasurable ways.

Apart from performing a personal analysis of your strengths and weaknesses, a great approach would be to gain insights from close friends or family members. For example, you might want to ask a dear friend "Do you think I am rude?" The key is to be open to responses, limit excuses, and be honest with yourself to propel you toward your self-development goals.

No one has it all together. We all need to develop certain aspects of our lives. As you make your daily steps towards self-development do not be too hard on yourselves. Remember that even if you do not achieve all your objectives, growth has been achieved as there is now self-awareness and your purpose has been more clearly defined.

CHAPTER ONE TAKEAWAYS

- Self-Development involves taking the necessary steps to improve yourself.

- It is a lifelong process.

- It involves building strengths, overcoming weaknesses, and acquiring new knowledge, skills, and abilities.

- Self-Development works best when attention is given to your emotional, social, mental, spiritual, and physical being.

- The benefits are immeasurable!

Goal Setting: A Blueprint for Success

One of the first steps in self-development is goal setting. Goal setting is important as it helps you to define what you want to achieve and prioritize what is important. By setting goals, you can hold yourself accountable, build your confidence, track your journey, and increase your productivity.

As you set your goals, it is imperative to analyze the motive behind the goal to determine whether it is really what you want or whether you are doing it to please others. For example, a teenager who wants to pursue a career as an artist may feel pressured by family members to become a doctor and set goals accordingly to please the family. This could have a negative impact on the emotional area of self-development. Ask yourself questions such as "Why do I want to achieve this?", "How will it be beneficial to me?" "How does it align with my spiritual values" and "How will its fulfillment benefit others?"

Try to set both short and long-term goals and feel free to adjust them should the need arise. Breaking the larger goals into more attainable smaller goals will give you a sense of accomplishment upon completion. Furthermore, remember to reward yourself after achieving each goal.

The SMART method is a great tool for assisting you in your goal-setting process. The acronym SMART stands for *Specific, Measurable, Achievable, Realistic/ Relevant, and Timebound.* Using SMART goals propels you towards achieving your goals.

Specific – Clearly defined goals to lead to a plain path of success.

Measurable – The use of specific criteria to measure your progress helps you to determine if you are on track towards accomplishing your goals.

Achievable – Goals should push you out of your comfort zone but should not be beyond your reach.

Relevant/Realistic – Goals are relevant if they are aligned with your greater vision. Additionally, note that goals are realistic if you have the resources or the time to achieve them.

Time-Bound – Deadlines should be set, beginning of course with a start date.

The use of goal journals is a great way to record your progress on this journey. As you track your progress, you can adjust as necessary. Prioritize your goals to ensure you focus your attention on the most important tasks first. State precisely what you want, then write the necessary steps to attain them. Remember to relax when setting your goals; do not be too hard on yourself. Stay positive.

Using the information you obtained from your self-examination, set your goals to overcome your weaknesses and enhance your strengths. You can also use the SMART goals for any area in your life including planning vacations, improving your appearance, and retirement planning.

It is a great idea to use a portion of the journal for positive affirmations and to list your goals as if you have already accomplished them. For example, if as a part of your developmental objectives, you want to improve your communication skills, you may write in your journal "I now have no fear when speaking to crowds."

A fantastic tool to utilize in goal setting is the technique of visualization. Visualization is the act of imagining your goal is completed or that you have achieved your desire. What are some simple steps in the process of visualization? Focus on an image of a goal for a while without distraction. While you are doing this, if you see clues regarding steps towards achieving the goal, write them down and act on them. Focus on positive outcomes rather than negative distractions. If you are constantly thinking about negative outcomes, they will begin to manifest in your life. True prosperity begins in your mind. Dr. Robert Anthony revealed that "Whatever you give dominant thought to, whether it be sickness or health, success or failure, abundance or lack, love or hate, the object of your attention will be attracted to you."

A vision board is a fun way to believe in your goals. You may use a cork board, sticking board, cardboard, or even a scrapbook. Obtain pictures of your desired goals from magazines or online and stick them on your board or in your scrapbook. Look at your vision board daily or as often as possible and believe that you will obtain them. Use your five senses when visualizing. Give thanks in advance for achieving the goals. However, do not think the goals will materialize if you do not want to get out of bed or if you are paralyzed by fear. You must take action to see the results. As a Christian, I normally use pictures that I feel are following God's plans for my life. Remember to reinforce the visualization with positive affirmations such as those I will discuss in Chapter Nine.

When your desired goals begin to manifest, remember to place a design around the picture on the vision board to celebrate and be grateful for your achievements.

CHAPTER TWO TAKEAWAYS

- Goal setting can help you to define what you want to achieve and prioritize what is important.

- It is important to analyze the motive behind the goal.

- The SMART method is a great tool for assisting you in your goal-setting process. The acronym SMART stands for **S**pecific, **M**easurable, **A**chievable, **R**ealistic/Relevant, and **T**ime-Bound

- Visualization and positive affirmations are fantastic techniques for manifesting your dreams.

Developing Focus and Passion for Your Purpose

"The mind is not a vessel to be filled but a fire to be kindled" - Plutarch

It was the late Dr. Myles Munroe, the international motivational speaker, Kingdom leader, and best-selling author who said, "The greatest tragedy in life is not death, but a life without a purpose." Your purpose is the reason behind your existence. Many have asked questions such as, "What is the purpose of my life?" or "Why was I born?" An integral part of self-development is understanding the purpose of your life and focusing on fulfilling it. As you move with passion towards fulfilling your purpose, it may lead to feelings of self-worth, contentment, fulfillment, and wellness.

Mediocrity is Not an Option

Develop a passion for your purpose to steer and propel you towards its successful fulfillment. Put your all into completing goals regardless of how large or small the goal is. Continuously improve the process towards achieving these goals in whatever way you can think of. Do not settle for mediocrity and you must be disciplined and give the project everything you've got. Only a few people endure to the end; most people give up at the first hurdle. Make up your mind that you will not be one of those people. You must push yourself to get up even after failing and keep the goal and your overall life purpose in mind. Do your best to exceed expectations. In his book _"The Ultimate_

Secrets of Total Self Confidence", Dr. Robert Anthony stated, "The opposite of bravery is not cowardliness but conformity." You must decide whether you want to conform to what the crowd is doing and live a mediocre life or embrace your individuality and be all that you were created to be. The choice is up to you.

Regain your Passion

It may be difficult to feel passionate about something if your life has been stuck in a rut. Routines are important, however, sometimes they can prevent you from enjoying life to its fullest. Taking up a new hobby, meeting new friends, and reading new books, especially motivational ones, may be just what you need to regain some passion and fire back into your life.

Do not Overload Yourself

I believe that we all have a God-given purpose for our lives. It is imperative to avoid distractions in the fulfillment of that purpose. You may be multi-talented; however, identify one or two of your gifts and focus on enhancing them or you may end up being a "jack of all trades and master of none." It is okay to have many goals but place your passion and diligence in the pursuit of your divine purpose.

Procrastination

A serious hindrance to self-development is procrastination as it depletes you of your passion. You may be all fired up when you begin a project but after delaying the process all that fire tends to dry up. Distractions such as watching unproductive things on television waste valuable time. Exert your efforts on achieving your goals rather than burning yourself out doing things that you and those close to you will not benefit from. A few **tips** for avoiding procrastination include the following:

- Get others involved to hold you accountable.

- Prioritize and accomplish the most important objective first.

- Allocate adequate time for each project.

- Work in increments to avoid feeling overwhelmed.

So, get passionate about your self-development, completing your goals, and most importantly fulfilling the divine purpose for your life.

CHAPTER THREE TAKEAWAYS

- An integral part of self-development is understanding the purpose of your life and focusing on fulfilling it.
- Choose not to live a mundane or mediocre life.
- Procrastination depletes you of your passion and should be avoided at all costs.
- Focus on your goals rather than mere distractions.

"Beloved, I pray that in all things thou mayest prosper and be in health, even as thy soul prospereth". 3 John 2-4 ASV

Focusing on areas of self-development such as your career, finances, and relationships could be very challenging if you are at the same time dealing with health issues. For example, if you became financially stable, however, time was not spent developing your mental or physical health, your finances may, at some point, be negatively affected. Your emotional and physical health are important factors in self-development. Self-care involves exercise, healthy diets, mental health, and many other areas. In this chapter, we will discuss some habits that could positively impact your overall well-being.

Eat a Nutritious Diet

The importance of a well-balanced diet cannot be overemphasized. The body needs essential vitamins, nutrients, and minerals to operate at its optimum.

The following is a list of dietary guidelines for our daily diet recommended by the American Dietetic Association (ADA):

- **Bread, Cereal, Rice & Pasta Group** / 6-11 servings
- **Fruit Group** / 2-4 servings
- **Vegetable Group** / 3-5 Servings
- **Meat, Poultry, Fish, Dry Beans, Eggs & Nuts Group** / 2-3 servings

- **Milk, Yogurt & Cheese Group** / 2- 3 servings

- **Fats, Oils & Sweets** / Use sparingly

It is time to throw away the junk food and get some real food into your body!

Some tips for maintaining a well-balanced diet include:

- Avoid fast foods as these contain a lot of sugars and saturated fats.

- Eat lots of green vegetables, whole grains, chicken, fish, and fruit.

- Include supplements such as vitamins, minerals, and nutrients.

- Limit the use of alcoholic beverages and salt.

- Drink lots of water to avoid dehydration.

- Steer clear of foods high in cholesterol, carbohydrates, saturated and trans fats.

- Avoid snacking between meals.

- Remove the skin from the chicken and eat as much lean meat as possible.

Take Time to Pamper Yourself

You must add some 'me' time to your schedule. "What is 'me' time?", you may ask. Me time is time to pamper yourself and treat yourself like the King or Queen you are! This can involve visiting a manicurist or pedicurist, obtaining a massage, changing your hairstyle, obtaining a facial, or doing whatever you feel like to improve your appearance. Sometimes when we look better, we feel better and obtain more compliments which tend to boost our confidence even more. Live a balanced life. So many people focus so much on their children, careers, spouse, or friends that they somehow lose themselves in the process.

Exercise

Walk, run, join a gym, purchase home gym equipment, or do whatever fits your lifestyle to keep physically fit. Of course, you would do this following the recommendations of health care providers. Exercising energizes you and assists in making you look and feel better. It also improves the function of certain organs and systems of our body such as our heart and lungs. Remember to include stretching exercises to promote increased flexibility, cardiovascular conditioning, and resistance exercises to improve endurance. Be committed to your routine and if possible, exercise for approximately half an hour a day.

Reduce Stress

Stress reduction may allow you to regain the passion and ability to focus on accomplishing your goals. Stress often leads to depression, health issues and problems with our immune system, fatigue, and sleeplessness. Some of the techniques that may assist you in coping with stress include listening to music you enjoy, asking for help, praying, exercising, taking up a hobby, reading a motivational book, or spending time with dear friends or loved ones who encourage you.

Develop a Positive Attitude

In his book "Attitude 101: What every leader needs to know" leadership expert, John C. Maxwell stated that attitude "is the prophet of our future".

A person's attitude is indeed a forecast of whether success or failure is ahead for a person. The famous salesman and Motivational Speaker, Zig Ziglar remarked in his famous quote that "It's your attitude, not your aptitude that will determine your altitude". The right attitude that is not unforgiving, overly critical, jealous, or arrogant, can take you farther than you can imagine. Many people are unable to maintain healthy relationships and jobs because of terrible attitudes. It is very important to develop a pattern of thinking that is positive rather than negative.

It was also stated by John C. Maxwell that "For some reason, many people think it's chic to be negative. I suspect that they think it makes them appear smart or important. But the truth is that a negative attitude hurts rather than helps the person who has it." No one wants to be around a chronic complainer or an argumentative person. If you are constantly having negative thoughts, it may lead to low self-esteem and attract more negative things into your life.

A healthy attitude places more value on people than things, is empathetic, positive, compassionate, displays temperance, self-confidence, and is grateful. If you are constantly having negative thoughts, it may lead to low self-esteem and attract more negative things into your life.

CHAPTER FOUR TAKEAWAYS

- Your emotional and physical health are important factors in self-development.

- The body needs essential vitamins, nutrients, and minerals to operate at its optimum.

- Take time to pamper yourself and remember to live a balanced life.

- Your attitude attracts negative or positive things into your life.

Catapulting Your Self Esteem

"Be yourself; everyone else is taken." -Oscar Wilde

If you are serious about your self-development, you must assess your self-esteem. Do you constantly speak negatively about yourself? Do you always feel inferior to others? Do you always believe others think they are better than you? These are common signs of low self-esteem. Other signs may include constant complaining and fault finding, boasting, the need for attention, people-pleasing, self-pity, and overindulgence which is often engaged in to compensate for weaknesses. Low self-esteem affects both young and old, rich, and poor.

You are unique. Everyone was created with a gift or talent. Many people discount their gift and wish they had the gift of another. They envy others and always want what others have because of a scarcity mentality or low self-esteem. Do not try to gain something at another person's expense. If you have an abundance mindset, you will know that there is more than enough to go around.

Take a closer look at your strengths and think of ways you can develop them. Colonel Saunders was talented in producing a seasoning for his chicken that was "finger-licking good" and look how he prospered because of focusing on that gift instead of trying to be someone else.

You will be surprised how many people who appear to be successful have low self-esteem. Many individuals, including teenagers, constantly speak negative things about themselves. "I'm so stupid", I sometimes hear them say. Always speak positively about yourself; this is not being arrogant. The words you speak have a spiritual impact and manifest in many ways. Arrogance occurs when someone exaggerates their importance. Building your self-esteem also encourages others to value you and leads to favorable outcomes for you. Opportunities you may have declined due to a lack of self-confidence you happily embrace. In your self-development journey, you must destroy low self-esteem.

You may feel like you are a failure because of mistakes you have made in the past and losses you may have experienced but remember that every obstacle you have faced can be used to teach an important lesson and often have hidden opportunities. If, for example, you were emotionally hurt by a toxic relationship, you may learn life lessons that will teach you what to avoid in the next relationship, and next time you may meet Mr. or Mrs. Right! So do not give up after disappointments; they only occurred to strengthen you and better is coming. You have what it takes to grow, develop, succeed, and overcome.

A few tips to catapult your self-esteem include:

- Use positive affirmations.
- Set boundaries in the way others treat you.
- Learn to say "no".
- Do not criticize yourself.
- Make a list of your strengths and look at it often.
- Do not compare yourself with others.
- Do not be too hard on yourself; laugh.

- Help others.

- Take care of your appearance.

CHAPTER FIVE TAKEAWAYS

- The words you speak have a spiritual impact and manifest either positively or negatively in your lives.

- Allow adversities to strengthen you; know better is coming.

- Utilize techniques such as setting boundaries, speaking positive affirmations, and other methods discussed in the chapter to boost your self-esteem.

Maintaining Healthy Relationships

"There is nothing on this earth more to be prized than true friendship." -St. Thomas Aquinas

Your self-development would be incomplete without an analysis of the state of your relationships. Healthy relationships can promote peace of mind, increase opportunities through networking, decrease stress, positively affect your physical and mental health, and lead to overall development.

Relationships

Having at least three **genuine** friends in your life is important. Quality friends are vital as research has shown that they can improve your health, inspire you, make you happier, help you to be more prosperous, and productive, and improve your self-esteem.

Toxic friendships, on the other hand, can increase your chances for substance abuse, depression, obesity, and other vices. As Dr. Myles Munroe stated, "The law of association states that you become like those with whom you spend time."

According to Vanessa Van Edwards, bestselling author, internationally acclaimed speaker, and founder of Science of People, "research has shown that the average person has 3 to 5 very close friends, 10 to 15 people in their circle, and 100 to 150 acquaintances in their social network.

Naturally, these numbers can vary widely based on your personality, career, location, and social skills".

Before establishing close friendships or romantic relationships, it is important to know what constitutes quality relationships.

1. **Trust** – A quality friend is trustworthy and will not reveal your secrets and weaknesses or gossip about you. There is loyalty and allegiance.
2. **Reciprocates** – The relationship will not be one-sided. For example, the kindness you exhibit to them will be returned to you.
3. **Boundaries are respected** – Your time and the boundaries you have expressed to them are respected.

4. **Accepted for who you are** – You are not belittled for your characteristics, attributes, or appearance.

5. **Encouragement is given** – They inspire, motivate, and uplift you to be a better you. They also empower you to be all that you can be.

6. **Offer support** – They are present in your life offering assistance during times of adversity and celebrating in those seasons when you celebrate.

7. **A joy to be around** – You have fun when they are around rather than feeling burdened.

8. **Offer constructive criticism** – Rather than criticizing for no reason, they offer constructive criticism from a heart that is willing to inspire you and always displays kindness and compassion towards you.

<u>*What Constitutes an Unhealthy Friendship?*</u>

Certain characteristics are sometimes evident in unhealthy relationships.

1. Physical or mental abuse, betrayal, disrespect, feelings of being used, manipulation, loss of passion.
2. Mocking and ridicule.
3. Wrong judgments for the situation you are in rather than helping.
4. Secrecy. An example of this is when someone can only reveal their feelings for you in private but in public is distant.

<u>*Tips for Attracting and Maintaining Healthy Friendships*</u>

1. Pray for discernment to identify the true motives of individuals.

2. Spend quality time with friends and partners. It is important to live a balanced life. If excessive time and attention are spent in a certain area such as a career, you may eventually find yourself without friends or a partner.

3. Communicate in a supportive way. Do not dominate the communication; listen attentively to what the other person has to say.

4. Develop empathy for others understanding cultural differences and the impact of past experiences on their lives.

5. Do not be afraid to express your needs and what you like and do not like. In the same manner, avoid as much as possible those things that may cause your partner pain and try to do the things that please them. Small

gestures, such as birthday gifts, can have a big impact.

6. If an argument occurs, focus on identifying the problem and finding a solution, rather than belittling or lashing out at the individual.

Icebreakers

Do you have difficulty starting a conversation to meet new friends? Why not ask questions such as,

- *Are you having fun?*
- *How long have you known the hostess?*
- Have you been here before?
- The food looks great. I'm not sure what to select. Do you have any suggestions?

Other options for conversation icebreakers include:

- *Paying a compliment.*

- *Remarking on a topic the person seems passionate about.*

- *Mentioning something about the weather.*

The use of the F.O.R.D. method is a terrific way to ask meaningful questions when you meet someone and wish to build a rapport with them. F.O.R.D. is an acronym that stands for **Family, Occupation, Recreation, and Dreams**. The acronym reminds you of certain areas you can focus on to ask questions. An example for each area follows:

Family: "Are you a part of a large family?"

Occupation: "What do you like most about your career?"

Recreation: "If you had more free time and money, what would you be doing right now?"

Dreams: "If you could travel anywhere, where would you like to visit?"

Teams

Developing the ability to work effectively in teams has many benefits such as increased productivity, personal growth, reduced feelings of being overwhelmed and burnt out, receiving new ideas from brainstorming, and gaining conflict resolution skills. Teams may also promote diversity and inclusion. It was President Woodrow Wilson who declared "We should not only use all the brains we have but all that we can borrow."

There are some skills you would need to develop to work in teams including critical thinking, delegation, listening, time management, problem-solving, collaboration, and communication skills.

CHAPTER SIX TAKEAWAYS

- Healthy relationships can promote peace of mind, increase opportunities through networking, decrease stress, positively affect your physical and mental health and lead to overall development.

- It is important to have at least three quality friends in your life.

- Effective communication skills are foundational to all relationships.

- It is essential to know what constitutes healthy and toxic friendships.

- Use the F.O.R.D. (Family, Occupation, Recreation, Dreams) technique to start meaningful connections.

Developing Intellectually

"The most useless are those who never change through the years." -James M. Barrie

The intellectual mind and in particular, education are key elements of self-development. It was stated by the first President of South Africa, and Anti-Apartheid Activist, Nelson Mandala that

"Education is the great engine of personal development. It is through education that the daughter of a peasant can become a doctor, that the son of a mine worker can become the head of the mine, that a child of farm workers can become the president of a great nation. It is what we make out of what we have, not what we are given, that separates one person from another."

<u>*The Importance of Education*</u>

- Increases critical thinking skills.

- Opens doors of opportunities.

- Broadens the mind and helps you to be more compassionate and tolerant of others.

- Identifies areas you are gifted in and areas of weakness.

- Improves your skills, knowledge, and abilities.

- Improves the chances of earning a good salary.

<u>*Learning Opportunities*</u>

If you are unable to attend college or university at this time, there are many opportunities that you can still embrace to better equip yourself. There are many free online courses available in most subject areas. Additionally, it is truly amazing how much you can learn nowadays just by watching YouTube videos on various topics. Attending a short certificate course or watching online Webinars are also great options for self-development. Subscribing to various informative magazines or joining a club and attending conferences associated with your goals can also allow you to enjoy yourself while networking and growing educationally.

CHAPTER SEVEN TAKEAWAYS

- Education can broaden your mind and increase your chances of opportunities.

- In addition to traditional means of educating yourself such as face-to-face attendance at colleges and universities, there are now countless ways that you can better equip yourself in today's world of technology such as by attending online classes, or by watching online Webinars, and YouTube tutorial videos.

An Abundance of Gratitude

"We can complain because rose bushes have thorns or rejoice because thorn bushes have roses." -Abraham Lincoln

Gratitude is a key to obtaining more in life. It is important to develop an attitude of gratitude. When you are grateful for what you have, you often obtain more of what you desire. For example, if I gave my daughter $50 and she took the money and complained and said I was cheap because I did not give her $100, do you think I would quickly give her $100. I think not. Being grateful leads to receiving more.

Just a few of the areas you can be grateful for are the individuals in your life, your possessions, and your accomplishments. Be thankful for good and bad experiences because all of this helps to strengthen you and make you wiser. Be thankful even for the things you have yet to achieve. For example, if one of your goals is to obtain your dream home, one of your affirmations might be "I am thankful for my dream home that is two-story, with large walk-in closets, spacious rooms, in a safe neighborhood, and with friendly neighbors". Make your affirmation concerning the home as plain as possible and give thanks for it before it even arrives! Or maybe you need genuine friends in your life. Perhaps your affirmation can be "I am so thankful for my loyal friends who are there for me and assistance in good and bad times." Try making a list of things for which you are grateful.

Gratitude is very energizing. Too much negativity depletes your strength and limits progress or development.

CHAPTER EIGHT TAKEAWAYS

- Gratitude is a key to obtaining more in your life.

- Make it a point of being thankful for your desire in advance of achieving it.

- Make a list of the things you are grateful for

- Gratitude is energizing.

"For success attitude is equally important as ability." -Walter Scott

There are times when you may feel discouraged and wish you had someone who would offer words to encourage you but instead all you receive are negative comments and criticism. Words are commonly used as a weapon to belittle, destroy, and judge rather than to motivate, validate, support, heal, and build.

Instead of waiting for others to validate you, positive affirmations can reenergize you as there is profound power in spoken words. Speak life rather than death into your situation. Below are a few positive statements you can use but feel free to create some of your own.

1.   *I am loved, valued, and worthy of love*

2.   *I am courageous*

3.   *All I hear is good news*

4.   *I am unstoppable by the Grace of God*

5.   *Money is flowing into my hands like a river*

6.   *Abundance is always in my life*

7.   *I am developing spiritually, intellectually, emotionally, financially, physically, and in my relationships*

8.   *I am blessed and favored by others*

9.   *I am unstoppable by the grace of God*

10. *I constantly receive favor from all sides*

11. *I am successful*

12. *I am victorious and optimistic*

13. *I am walking in divine health*

14. *I am experiencing promotions and increase*

15. *Everything I put my hands to prospers*

16. *All I have are positive thoughts; negative thoughts do not cloud my mind*

17. *My surroundings are peaceful*

18. *I have loyal, devoted friends who are there for me in times of need*

19. *My perspective is important*

20. *It is okay for me to say no and to set boundaries*

21. *I am a money magnet*

22. *I deserve to be treated with respect and dignity*

23. *I am a quick thinker*

24. *I receive my requests speedily*

25. *I am in my season of blessings and increases, not losses*

26. *I am shielded on all sides by the mercies and favor of God*

27. *I forgive myself for past mistakes*

28. *I am beautiful in my way*

29. *I am fulfilling the purpose of my life*

30. *I am grateful*

31. *I am loved*

32. *I am full of wisdom, knowledge, and understanding*

CHAPTER NINE TAKEAWAY

- Speak life rather than death into your situation by using positive affirmations.

- Instead of waiting for others to encourage you, encourage yourself by saying positive things about yourself and your future.

Spiritual Development

"As long as you live, keep learning how to live." -Seneca

Spiritual development is one of the most important components of Self Development. There is a purpose for which you were created. Without knowing your purpose, the goals you set in your life may be aimless and pointless. Self-Development for Christians is a channel for discovering the purpose of God for our lives, serving God, and being good stewards of the spiritual gifts he has given to us by maximizing our potential.

To grow spiritually you must read your holy book which is The Bible for Christians. From this book, you will obtain many of your values, and beliefs and gain insight into the good qualities you should sustain and the bad characteristics you need to discard. Additionally, it will assist you in determining how to conduct yourself during any circumstances. Introspection or self-examination must take place as you read and pray during which time you can look closely at your thoughts, feelings, beliefs, and motivations.

Finally, growing spiritually involves a deepening relationship with God, purifying of motives, developing of character, and a better relationship with your fellowmen.

CHAPTER TEN TAKEAWAYS

- Spiritual development is one of the most important components of Self Development,

- Without knowing your purpose, the goals you set in your life may be aimless and pointless.

- Self-Development for Christians is a channel for discovering the purpose of God for our lives, serving God, and being good stewards of the spiritual gifts he has given to us by maximizing our potential.

Thank you for reading the book "***Self-Development Strategies: The Five-Minute Guide to A Better You***". I would love to hear some feedback from you! Whenever you purchase this book, please write a review of the book to tell me what you think about it. I am always striving to please you more.

The information in this book is not intended as a substitute for professional advice, emergency treatment, or formal first-aid training. It is designed to provide information and motivation to readers. It is sold with the understanding that the author and publisher are not engaged to render any type of psychological, legal, or another kind of professional advice. The author and publisher shall not be liable for any physical, psychological, emotional, financial, or commercial damages, including, but not limited to, special, incidental consequential, or other damages. Do not use this information to diagnose or develop a treatment plan for a health problem or disease without consulting a qualified health care provider if you are in a life-threatening or emergency medical situation, seek medical assistance immediately.

Anthony, D. R. (1984). *The Ultimate Secrets of Self Confidence.* San Diego, CA: The Berkley Publishing Group.

Best 100 Public Domain Quotes of all Times - Collection 01. (2022). Retrieved from The Golden Quotes.Net: https://www.thegoldenquotes.net/best-100-public-domain-quotes-of-all-time-collection-01/

Best 100 Public Domain Quotes of All Times Collection 1. (2022). Retrieved from The Golden Quotes.Net: https://www.thegoldenquotes.net/best-100-public-domain-quotes-of-all-time-collection-01/

CFI Team. (2022, May 7). *What are SMART Goals?* Retrieved from Corporate Finance Institute: https://corporatefinanceinstitute.com/resources/knowledge/other/smart-goal/

Clark, K. (2021, February 28). *5 Areas of Self Development.* Retrieved from Gen Twenty (The Twenty Something Guide to Life): https://gentwenty.com/areas-of-personal-development/#:~:text=There%20are%20several%20different%20topics,spiritual%2C%20emotional%2C%20and%20physical.

Edwards, V. V. (2022). *57 Killer Conversation Starters.* Retrieved from Science of People: https://www.scienceofpeople.com/conversation-starters-topics/

Edwards, V. V. (2022). *7 Science-Backed Reasons Why Friends are Important.* Retrieved from Science of People: https://www.scienceofpeople.com/friends-important/

Goal Setting. (2022). Retrieved from CALE Learning
    Enhancement - Eastern Washington University:
    https://inside.ewu.edu/calelearning/psychological-
    skills/goal-setting/

Indeed Editorial Team. (2021, September 30). *The
    Advantages of Working in A Team*. Retrieved from
    Indeed: https://uk.indeed.com/career-advice/career-
    development/advantages-of-working-in-a-team

Indeed Editorial Team. (2022, May 23). *13 Ways to Start a
    Conversation*. Retrieved from Indeed:
    https://www.indeed.com/career-advice/career-
    development/how-to-start-a-conversation

Maxwell, J. C. (2003). *Attitude 101: What Every Leader
    Needs to Know*. Nashville, Tennessee: Thomas
    Nelson, Inc.

Maxwell, J. C. (2003). *Relationships 101: What Every
    Leader Needs to Know*. Nashville, Tennessee:
    Thomas C. Nelson, Inc.

Maxwell, J. C. (2008). *Teamwork 101: What Every Leader
    Needs to Know*. Nashville, Tennessee: Thomas
    Nelson, Inc.

Mindnatic. (2022). *How to Talk to Anyone and Everyone*.
    Mindnatic.

Munroe, D. M. (2003). *The Principles and Power of Vision*.
    New Kensington, PA: Whitaker House.

Munroe, D. M. (2014). *The Power of Character in
    Leadership*. New Kensington, PA: Whitaker House.

Nyatyowa, L. (2017, June 19). *4 Reasons Why Personal
    Development Should be A Priority*. Retrieved from
    Oxford Academy:
    https://www.oxbridgeacademy.edu.za/blog/4-
    reasons-personal-development-priority/

Pratt, A. C. (2020). *I'm Loving My Age: A Believer's Guide
    to Aging Gracefully and Words of Hope for the
    Elderly*. Maitland, FL: Xulon Press.

Take Charge of Your Personal Development. (2020, November 20). Retrieved from Harappa Diaries: https://harappa.education/harappa-diaries/personal-or-self-development/

www.ingramcontent.com/pod-product-compliance
Lightning Source LLC
Chambersburg PA
CBHW050803160726

48004CB00002B/679